Action for the Environment

Transportation Solutions

Daniel Gilpin

Smart Apple Media

First published in 2004 by Franklin Watts
96 Leonard Street, London EC2A 4XD

Franklin Watts Australia
45-51 Huntley Street, Alexandria NSW 2015

Editor: Adrian Cole, Design: Proof Books, Art
Director: Jonathan Hair, Picture Researcher: Kathy
Lockley

Acknowledgements
© Airbus, 2004, All rights reserved - Proprietary
Information. Photo by H. Gousse 14 t, 14 b, 15. Martin
Barlow/Art Directors & TRIP Photo Library 29b. Hans
Blossey/Still Pictures 2, 11. Martin. Bond/Still Pictures 13 t.
Adrian Cole 16, 31. Vicki Coombs/Ecoscene 13 b. Stephen
Coyne/Ecoscene 22 t. Ron Giling/Still Pictures 5, COVER
TL. Richard Glover/Ecoscene 1, 10. Russell Gordon/Still
Pictures 8. © Greenheart Project/Mr. Seiichi Kunikata 17 b.
Nick Hawkes/Ecoscene 24. David Hoey/Art Directors &
TRIP Photo Library 25 b. ITDG/Rachel Berger 7.
N.A.S.A./Tom Tschida 26–27. Tony Page/Ecoscene 4,
COVER B. Rex Features 28. Ray Roberts/Ecoscene COVER
TR. Helene Rogers/Art Directors & TRIP Photo Library 19 t.
J. Sainsbury plc 9. Hartmut Schwarzbach/Still Pictures 22
b. Copyright © 2001-2003 Segway LLC 29 t. Ulrich
Sonntag/Greenpeace 21. Friedrich Stark/Still Pictures 19 b.
Jochen Tack/Still Pictures 17 t. U.S. DOE Photo 6 t, 12, 18,
20, 23, 25 t, 27 b. Virgin Trains/Milepost 92-1/2 6 b.

Published in the United States by Smart Apple Media
2140 Howard Drive West, North Mankato,
Minnesota 56003

Library of Congress Cataloging-in-Publication Data

Gilpin, Daniel.
Transportation solutions / by Daniel Gilpin.
p. cm. — (Action for the environment)
Includes index.
ISBN 1-58340-599-2
1. Transportation—Environmental aspects—
Juvenile literature. I. Title. II. Series.

HE147.65.G55 2005
388—dc22   2004059198

9 8 7 6 5 4 3 2 1

Contents

World in motion   4

Transportation networks   6

Reducing car use   8

Driving to work   10

Public transportation   12

Taking to the skies   14

On the water   16

Transporting goods   18

Fuel efficiency   20

Cleaner fuel   22

Electric power   24

Solar and magnetic power   26

Traveling into the future   28

Glossary   30

Find out more   31

Index   32

World in motion

The transportation we use makes up an important part of our lives. But some forms of transportation are more harmful to the environment than others are. By thinking about the transportation we use and how often we use it, we can help to protect the environment around us.

FOSSIL FUEL POLLUTION

Most engines in cars, trains, boats, and airplanes use gasoline or other fossil fuels. These fuels generate energy when they are burned in an engine. Unfortunately, this process also produces carbon dioxide and other polluting "greenhouse" gases that damage the environment. People are now trying to do more to reduce these emissions.

Cars and other vehicles that use fossil fuels produce high levels of greenhouse gas emissions.

Bike riders in Beijing, China. In busy cities, biking is often the fastest way to travel short distances.

Action stations

Most forms of transportation have a negative effect on the environment, but there are two that have no impact at all. Walking and biking are completely environmentally friendly. The only energy they use is the energy produced by our own bodies. In addition to being good for the environment, walking and biking are great forms of exercise that can help keep us healthy.

GLOBAL WARMING

High levels of carbon dioxide are thought to be the main cause of global warming. As the gas builds up in the air (see right), it traps more and more heat from the sun—like the panes of glass in a greenhouse—warming Earth's atmosphere and affecting the climate. Most scientists predict that if this continues, more of us will experience extreme weather such as droughts and storms.

heat from the sun

atmosphere containing greenhouse gases

some heat is trapped and warms up the atmosphere

Transportation networks

The networks on which vehicles travel also affect the environment. Roads, railroads, and canals help people and goods move around easily. Unfortunately, they often cut through natural habitats and disturb the environment.

Building a new road. The asphalt used to make some roads stops plants from growing on them and prevents rainwater from reaching the ground.

ROADS

Roads generally have a bigger impact on the environment than any other transportation network. Every year, thousands of people and animals are killed crossing roads. Many anti-road campaigners are trying to encourage people to use other transportation networks, such as railroads. They also want to prevent more roads from being built, particularly in the developed world.

RAILROADS

Railroads have a relatively small impact on the environment because the trains they carry produce less pollution than cars and trucks. Railroads usually blend into the environment—their embankments may actually become havens for wildlife. More cities, such as Kuala Lumpur in Malaysia, are building monorail or "light railway" networks to help reduce congestion on roads.

Railroads and canals have a small environmental impact.

CANALS

In a few places, canals are still used to transport people and goods. The barges that travel on canals move slowly and quietly and hardly disturb wildlife at all. Many canals actually provide homes for plants, waterbirds, and other animals.

Women in Sri Lanka preparing a new road. Small-scale projects like this improve links to markets and services.

Action stations

Some countries in the developing world have very poor transportation networks, which increases poverty levels. Many rural roads consist of narrow dirt tracks that prevent people from traveling to buy food and collect water. The Intermediate Technology Development Group (ITDG) has helped local women in Mulberigama, Sri Lanka, build three-quarters of a mile (1.2 km) of gravel road. This small-scale project will have a minimal impact on the environment and will greatly improve people's lives. The road will be used mainly by nonmotorized transportation methods, such as bicycles and animal-drawn carts.

Reducing car use

Most families in the developed world have a car, and many have more than one. Although cars can be useful, they are often used far more than is necessary.

These school children in Hong Kong are walking to school. Many people make trips in cars that could easily be made on foot.

THE TRIP TO SCHOOL

Thousands of parents drive their children to and from school, which saves them time. But these trips are usually short. If more children walked or took the bus to school, it would reduce car emissions and cut road congestion.

DRIVING TO THE STORE

Many people use their cars to go shopping because there is often too much to carry. But driving to the store to buy one or two things causes unnecessary pollution. Walking or biking is often just as easy—and much healthier and cheaper, too.

Action stations

Many people get into their cars without thinking. Cutting down on unnecessary trips is one of the easiest ways to reduce pollution and the damage it causes. Many people hope that Internet shopping will change the way people buy goods. Those who have access to the Internet can shop online at supermarkets, music retailers, and clothing stores without going anywhere near a car. The goods are then delivered by a van that makes several deliveries in one trip.

Groceries delivered to your door. Services like this could cut pollution by reducing the number of trips people make to the store.

Driving to work

More people use cars to get to and from work than for any other reason. These trips often cause congestion and are the main source of pollution in most towns and cities. They are trips that have to be made, but there are ways to reduce the problems they cause.

A traffic jam in Bangkok, Thailand. Some governments are trying new ways to reduce the levels of pollution caused by road traffic (see right).

TRAFFIC JAMS

Many workers around the world spend hours every month stuck in traffic jams. Even when cars are not moving, the engines use fuel and create pollution. To reduce unnecessary pollution, traffic experts recommend that drivers turn their engines off if they do not move for more than two minutes. Some new types of car engines do this automatically!

WORKING FROM HOME

Today, more and more people in the developed world have an opportunity to work from home. By using computers and the Internet, they can communicate with people around the world. Some people never have to go to an office at all. Working from home saves travel time and money and brings pollution levels down because it reduces the number of trips made each day.

Carpool lanes on highways like this could encourage people to travel together.

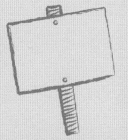

Action stations

Unfortunately, many people have no choice but to drive to work. To meet new environmental laws, governments have come up with plans to help reduce the pollution and congestion these trips cause. One simple way is for people to travel to work together. Cities in the United States have introduced carpool lanes on many roads—there are now 125 such projects in 30 states. These lanes are only open to cars with two or more people in them and are monitored by special traffic cameras. Carpool lanes are almost always less busy than other lanes, so people using them benefit from shorter travel times.

Public transportation

For most people, the main alternative to traveling by car is to use public transportation. Buses, trolleys, and trains offer a wide range of services over long and short distances. These forms of transportation do less damage to the environment than cars and are safer, too.

BUSES

For many people, buses are the most convenient way to travel. They produce far less pollution than cars, even though they have bigger engines. This is because each bus can carry the same number of passengers as would fill several cars. Some cities have introduced buses that produce even lower emissions (see page 23).

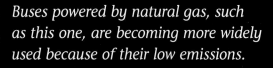

Buses powered by natural gas, such as this one, are becoming more widely used because of their low emissions.

TRAINS AND TROLLEYS

Trains are one of the most environmentally friendly or "green" forms of transportation. An average train can carry as many as 1,000 passengers at a time, using the power from a single engine. Some trains are powered by electricity, making them even greener. Trolleys operate in urban areas and are usually powered by electricity. They have fewer cars and travel over shorter distances than trains.

A trolley in Strasbourg, France. Trolleys are ideal for traveling around a busy city.

Action stations

Some governments in countries with busy cities have found ways to encourage people to get out of their cars and onto public transportation. Drivers in Singapore, Melbourne, and London have to pay a toll or charge if they want to use particular roads downtown. People on public transportation do not have to pay the charge. These plans have reduced the number of vehicles on the roads in these cities by about 15 percent.

Entering the congestion charge zone in London. Plans like this reduce the number of vehicles on the road and encourage people to use public transportation.

Taking to the skies

As air travel becomes more affordable, larger numbers of people are choosing to fly between cities or to travel abroad. The global increase in air traffic is having a major impact on the environment because airplanes use massive amounts of fuel.

Huge airplane engines like this use vast amounts of fuel.

FLYING GAS GUZZLERS

For each mile traveled, a large airplane uses more fuel than 300 cars. These airplanes travel thousands of miles every few hours and have fuel tanks that carry 165 tons (150 t) at a time. As this fuel is burned, it produces huge amounts of carbon dioxide and other greenhouse gases. These gases are released into the upper atmosphere.

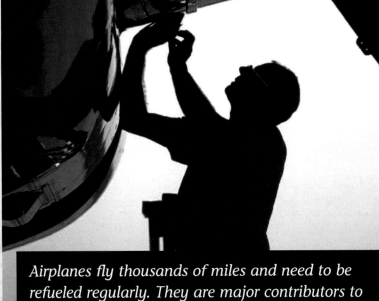

Airplanes fly thousands of miles and need to be refueled regularly. They are major contributors to high carbon dioxide levels in the atmosphere.

WINGS OF CHANGE

Modern airplanes are not very fuel efficient. Engineers dream of aircraft that will fly much faster and use a lot less fuel. One idea being considered is for specially designed airplanes that would fly just outside Earth's atmosphere—in space. These airplanes would be propelled using liquid hydrogen and would only produce harmless water vapor emissions.

Action stations

Airplane manufacturers are reducing the damage that their airplanes do to the environment. For example, since the 1970s, Airbus has reduced the fuel consumption of its planes by 40 percent. In 2004, officials at Airbus met with other companies and environmental experts at the Committee on Aviation Environmental Protection (CAEP) in Montreal, Canada. The CAEP is constantly working to meet new environmental laws, such as those controlling airplane noise and emission levels.

These airplanes are manufactured by Airbus. Although they use a lot of fuel, their fuel efficiency is slowly being improved.

On the water

In some parts of the world, people regularly travel by water. In coastal cities, ferries provide connections between islands and the mainland. Boats are also used to transport people along rivers, while oceangoing ships carry passengers to other countries.

ALL AT SEA

Oceangoing vessels, including ferries and cruise ships, can transport large numbers of passengers. But because of their large engines, they burn a lot of fuel and emit large quantities of greenhouse gases. To help reduce these emissions, many new ships are fitted with special combined gas and steam turbine electric engines. These engines are more fuel efficient and produce fewer emissions, making them better for the environment.

This ferry is one of many that carries commuters and tourists in and out of Sydney's Circular Quay in Australia.

ABOVE IT ALL

Some types of boats hardly touch the water at all. This lowers the amount of fuel needed to move the boat forward and reduces the amount of fossil fuel burned. Hydrofoils have underwater "wings" attached to legs on their hulls. These wings lift the boat out of the water when it is moving. Catamarans have two narrow hulls that move easily through the water.

This hydrofoil on the Yangtze River in China is faster and uses less fuel than a conventional boat.

Action stations

Not all boats use engines. Sailboats, for example, harness wind power to push them along. In Japan, the Greenheart Project is promoting the use of sail power to transport food aid and fairly traded goods around the world (see www.greenheartproject.org). Their new, environmentally friendly, small sail and solar-powered boat design does not use fuel, so it has an unlimited range. It can also carry larger loads than a motorized boat of a similar size because space is not taken up by an engine.

This is an illustration of the Greenheart Project boat, which could be used to transport goods. It has masts for the sails and a solar array to capture energy from the sun.

Transporting goods

Vehicles are not just used to move people around; they are also used to move goods. Almost everything we buy has been transported to the store from somewhere else. It may be produced nearby, but very often, it is brought in from far away.

IMPORTED GOODS

Some goods are brought in, or imported, from other countries. These goods are transported by road, air, rail, and sea. Transporting goods over long distances in trucks or airplanes uses large amounts of fossil fuel and creates a lot of pollution. More companies are being encouraged to use rail and sea transportation methods.

A train is perfect for transporting goods over a long distance. Most trains can move the same weight as about 30 trucks.

Food is transported to supermarkets from all over the world. Look for the labels on the fresh food shelves.

Action stations

Whenever possible, it is best to buy locally produced fruits and vegetables that have not been transported over long distances. This also applies to dairy products such as butter and cheese. These products have to be kept cold when being transported, which also uses a lot of energy.

ACCESSIBLE RAIL

Some environmental groups have joined forces with governments to reduce pollution. They aim to reduce the number of large container trucks on roads by making rail transportation more accessible and affordable to companies that produce or buy goods. Trucks will always be needed for trips between train stations and stores, but it is hoped that in the future they will make fewer long trips.

Unfortunately, most of the containers at this port will be collected by trucks.

Fuel efficiency

Virtually all vehicles on the road today are powered by gasoline or diesel fuel. However, some use much more fuel than others. Fuel efficiency can be improved to reduce the amount of fuel used by vehicles. This makes them more environmentally friendly because fewer emissions are produced.

Testing a solar-powered car in a wind tunnel. These cars must be as aerodynamic as possible. The same technology can be used to improve the shape of normal cars.

IMPROVING AERODYNAMICS

One way to improve fuel efficiency is to make a vehicle more aerodynamic. Cars with smooth lines and rounded edges cut through the air more easily as they travel, so they need less fuel to move them along. This is not only better for the environment but also saves the owner money.

SMALL IS BEAUTIFUL

In general, small cars use less fuel than larger cars. This is because small cars are lighter and use smaller engines to achieve similar speeds to those reached by large cars. Many governments set lower tax levels for small cars in an effort to encourage people to buy them instead of larger ones.

This amount of climate gas CO_2 (8 m³) is produced when you drive this car 100 km (6,7 l/100 km).

GREENPEACE

This amount of climate gas CO_2 (4 m³) is produced when you drive this car 100 km (3,3 l/100 km).

GREENPEACE

This Greenpeace demonstration shows that the SmILE car (yellow) produces fewer emissions than an unmodified car.

Action stations

The environmental group Greenpeace is concerned that the car manufacturing industry is not doing enough to reduce car emissions. They have developed a small, highly fuel-efficient car called SmILE (SMall, Intelligent, Light, and Efficient). The SmILE burns less than one gallon (3.5 l) of fuel per 60 miles (100 km). Greenpeace has also shown that by using technology available today, the fuel efficiency of most normal cars could be greatly improved.

Cleaner fuel

A lot has been done to reduce pollution caused by burning fossil fuels in vehicle engines. But many environmental groups would like the use of fossil fuels stopped completely. More is now being done to develop "cleaner" alternative fuels.

Many cars now run on cleaner alternative fuels, such as LPG (see right).

CUTTING EMISSIONS

Almost all gasoline is now unleaded because lead was shown to cause health problems. New, low-sulphur fuels are being introduced to reduce environmental damage, such as that caused by acid rain. Catalytic converters (cats) break down some chemicals in car emissions and are added to all new cars. Unfortunately, they do not reduce carbon dioxide levels.

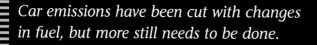

Car emissions have been cut with changes in fuel, but more still needs to be done.

ALTERNATIVE OPTIONS

There are cleaner fuels that can be used in place of gasoline and diesel. One is liquefied petroleum gas (LPG), which is already being used to power buses in many parts of the world. Another is liquid hydrogen, thought by many scientists to be the perfect replacement for gasoline. When hydrogen is burned, the main emission is water vapor, which is completely harmless.

Action stations

Biofuels, such as methanol and ethanol, are environmentally friendly fuels made from plant products, including vegetable oils. They are being used increasingly around the world because they are a source of renewable energy. Biofuel emissions are also less harmful than those produced by burning fossil fuels. Burning biofuels does produce carbon dioxide, but the crops used to generate biofuels take in carbon dioxide as they grow. This helps keep carbon dioxide levels in the atmosphere balanced.

This tractor in Texas is harvesting switchgrass, which will be used to produce biofuel.

Electric power

Some manufacturing companies are looking at other ways to solve the problem of vehicle emissions. One solution is to power vehicles by electric motors. Electric motors produce almost no pollution at all—especially if the electricity is generated by a renewable source.

RUNNING ON ELECTRICITY

Most electric motors are powered by electricity stored in batteries or electricity that runs along a rail or a power cable. They are used in electric trains and trolleys and can be found in countries around the world. Electrically powered cars are less common, but more are being developed. For example, in India, a company called Reva has developed a car that is powered by batteries that can be recharged from any household electrical outlet.

Electricity can be used to power a wide range of vehicles. However, most, such as this bus, rely on being able to recharge their batteries.

HYBRID ENGINES

Although electrically powered cars have improved, they can only travel short distances and are slower than traditional cars. New, hybrid engines use both gas and battery power. They are more fuel efficient and produce much lower greenhouse gas emissions than traditional cars. Honda and Toyota both make hybrid electric vehicles, and other companies, including General Motors, plan to introduce them in the near future.

This engineer is producing parts for a new engine. Improvements in technology have helped the development of affordable hybrid engines.

Action stations

There are a few places where electric vehicles are more common than gasoline vehicles, as well as some places where they are the only vehicles. On several small islands around the world, electric golf carts are the main form of transportation. Although they are small and slow, they are ideal for short trips. On Hong Kong's Lantau Island, for example, electric carts carry people through the small town of Discovery Bay. They also transport tourists and local people around the island of Caye Caulker off the coast of Belize.

This golf cart on Caye Caulker is perfect for carrying small loads around the island and does not produce any emissions.

Solar and magnetic power

Solar and magnetically powered vehicles are driven by electricity, and many designs are being tested. The technology is still expensive, but many people believe these vehicles could be the transportation solutions of the future.

HARNESSING THE SUN

Solar-powered vehicles use electricity that is generated by sunlight to drive electric motors. Although they only work during the day, some solar-powered cars can run at 50 miles (80 km) per hour using the same amount of energy as it takes to power a hair dryer. A solar-powered airplane developed by NASA holds the world record for flying higher than any other non-rocket-powered aircraft, at 18 miles (30 km) above Earth.

NASA's Helios solar-powered airplane has thousands of tiny solar cells built into its wings.

FLOATING ON AIR

Magnetically powered vehicles use electricity to generate powerful magnetic fields, which drive them along. Magnetic levitation (maglev) trains can reach speeds of 300 miles (500 km) per hour in almost complete silence. These trains do not produce any polluting emissions because they move without an engine.

Action stations

The first maglev train went into service in January 2004, when China officially opened its first maglev train line. The line links Pudong Airport to the city of Shanghai, about 20 miles (30 km) away. The new train transports passengers into the city in just longer than seven minutes—a fraction of the time it used to take by taxi or traditional train. If the new line turns out to be problem free and enough money can be found, the Chinese government plans to build another maglev link, this time between Shanghai and the capital city, Beijing.

At the moment, maglev trains are very expensive to build and run, but it is hoped that costs will come down in the future.

Traveling into the future

Transportation makes up such a large part of our lives that scientists and engineers are constantly trying to improve it. New transportation solutions must balance people's needs with environmental issues.

DRIVING CONCERNS

One of the biggest problems facing the developed world is the increasing number of cars on the roads. Instead of building new roads to reduce this congestion, environmental groups believe governments should invest more money in efficient public transportation to encourage people to stop using their cars.

Anti-road protests like this one are becoming increasingly common in the developed world. Many environmental campaigners argue that building more roads does not help to reduce traffic congestion or pollution.

Action stations

The Segway is a new form of personal transportation. It is capable of transporting one person over short distances in towns, where it may help reduce traffic pollution in the future. It has two wheels and is powered by battery-driven electric motors. The Segway may not solve the world's transportation problems, but it does suggest how future vehicles may look. It also shows that transportation solutions can be developed while keeping the environment in mind.

The Segway is just one idea that may reduce traffic pollution in towns and cities in the future.

INVESTING IN THE FUTURE

Affordable transportation solutions are needed in the developing world to reduce poverty and improve people's lives. One source of investment, the World Bank, has already assisted many countries by providing loans—although they must be paid back. In Brazil, railways were improved through the Brazil Railways Project and now generate money that can be reinvested in the network.

Transportation networks, such as this railroad in Brazil, need to be developed with people and the environment in mind.

Glossary

Acid rain Formed when sulphur dioxide and nitrogen oxides react in the atmosphere. Acid rain can make lakes acidic, poison animals and plants, and damage buildings.

Aerodynamic Shaped in a way that makes movement through air easier.

Atmosphere The layer of air that surrounds Earth.

Biofuels Liquid fuels, including ethanol, converted from organic materials.

Carbon dioxide The major greenhouse gas. Carbon dioxide is produced when fossil fuels are burned.

Catalytic converter (cat) A device attached to a car, which turns harmful exhaust gases into less toxic emissions.

Developed world The wealthier countries of the world, in which there are highly developed industries.

Developing world The poorer countries of the world, which rely more on farming than on industry.

Diesel A type of liquid fossil fuel, used to power some engines.

Efficiency A measure of how much energy a machine uses as it does its job. An efficient machine uses less energy than an inefficient machine.

Emissions Waste gases, such as carbon dioxide, and tiny particles of solids that are discharged by vehicle engines.

Fossil fuels Fuels such as coal, gas, or oil made from the fossilized remains of plants and animals. Burning fossil fuels produces the greenhouse gas carbon dioxide.

Global warming The gradual rise in Earth's temperature.

Greenhouse effect The effect of various "greenhouse" gases in Earth's atmosphere that trap the heat of the sun. Many greenhouse gases are made by human activities. Their increased production is thought to be raising global temperatures.

Greenhouse gases The gases that cause the greenhouse effect. The main ones are carbon dioxide, methane, and CFCs.

Intermediate Technology Development Group (ITDG) An organization founded in 1966 that works with local people to help find practical answers to poverty.

Lead A toxic metal produced by cars that do not run on unleaded gasoline. High amounts of lead in the air are dangerous.

Pollute To release harmful substances into the environment.

Renewable energy Energy supplies, such as wind energy and solar energy, that will never be used up. They cause little or no environmental damage.

Solar To do with the sun.

Sulphur dioxide A gas mostly produced when coal or oil is burned in power stations. It reacts in the atmosphere to form acid rain.

Tax Money that has to be paid to the government when something is bought or used.

World Bank An international organization that provides loans for development projects around the world.

Find out more

www.eere.energy.gov/afdc
The Web site for the U.S.-based Alternative Fuels Data Center is full of information on alternative fuels and the vehicles that use them.

www.epa.gov/globalwarming/kids
This site from the Environmental Protection Agency is packed with information on global warming and the greenhouse effect.

www.hybridcars.com
This Web site compares all of the hybrid cars currently on the market and includes a section on how hybrid engine technology works.

www.howstuffworks.com/maglev-train.htm
With the first maglev train now in operation, this site explains the technology that makes it work.

www.itdg.org
This site provides practical answers to poverty. To find out more about transportation solutions, click on the button at the top marked "Transport."

www.segway.com
Discover more about this remarkable new form of transportation and read stories written by people who own a Segway.

Index

A
acid rain 22, 30
aerodynamics 20, 30
airplanes 4, 14, 15, 26
alternative fuels 12, 22–23
anti-road campaigns 6, 28
atmosphere 5, 14, 15, 23, 30
Australia 16

B
bicycles 7
biking 5
biofuel 23, 30
boats 4, 7, 16, 17
Brazil 29
buses 8, 12, 23, 24

C
canals 6, 7
carbon dioxide 4, 5, 14, 22, 23, 30
carpool 11
cars 4, 8, 9, 10, 11, 13, 28
  design of 20
  electric 24, 25
  pollution by 6, 12
catalytic converter (cat) 22, 30
China 5, 17, 27
Committee on Aviation Environmental Protection (CAEP) 15
congestion 6, 8, 10, 11, 28
congestion charge 13

D
developed world 6, 11, 28, 30
developing world 7, 29, 30
diesel see also fossil fuels 20, 23, 30

E
electric power 13, 24–25, 26, 27, 29
emissions 4, 8, 12, 15, 20, 24

reducing 21, 22, 23, 25, 27, 30
engines 4, 10, 12, 16, 17, 21, 22, 27, 30
  hybrid 25, 31
ethanol 23, 30

F
ferries 16
fossil fuels 4, 18, 20, 21, 23, 30
fuel efficiency 15, 16, 20–21, 25, 30
fuel use or consumption 10, 14, 15, 16, 17, 20

G
gasoline see also fossil fuels 4, 20, 23, 25
  unleaded 22
global warming 5, 30
goods transportation 18–19
Greenheart Project, the 17
greenhouse effect 5, 30
greenhouse gases 4, 14, 16, 25, 30
Greenpeace 21

H, I, J
habitats 6
Hong Kong 8, 25
importing 18
India 24
Intermediate Technology Development Group (ITDG) 7, 30, 31
Internet access 11
Internet shopping 9
Japan 17

L, M, N
laws 11, 15
liquefied petroleum gas (LPG) 23
liquid hydrogen 15, 23

low sulphur fuel 22
magnetic power 26, 27
Malaysia 6
methanol 23
nonmotorized transportation 7

P, R
pollution 4, 8, 12, 18, 30
  reduction 9, 10, 11, 19, 22, 28, 29
public transportation 12–13, 28
railroads 6, 18, 19, 29
renewable energy 23, 24, 30
roads 6, 7, 13, 28

S
ships see boats
shopping 8, 9, 19
solar power or energy 17, 20, 26, 30
Sri Lanka 7
sulphur dioxide 22, 30

T
tax 21, 30
Thailand 10
toll roads 13
trains 4, 6, 12, 13, 18, 24, 27
transportation networks 6–7
traveling
  to school 8
  to the store 8–9
  to work 10–11
trolleys 12, 13, 24
trucks 6, 18, 19

U, W
U.S. 11, 23
walking 5, 8
wind power or energy 17, 30
World Bank, the 29, 30